AMICUS ILLUSTRATED • AMICUS INK

DO YOU REALLY WANT TO MEET
A KANGAROO?

WRITTEN BY CARI MEISTER   ILLUSTRATED BY DANIELE FABBRI

Amicus Illustrated and Amicus Ink
are imprints of Amicus
P.O. Box 1329
Mankato, MN 56002
www.amicuspublishing.us

Library of Congress Cataloging-in-Publication Data
Meister, Cari, author.
 Do you really want to meet a kangaroo? /
Cari Meister ; illustrated by Daniele Fabbri.
    pages cm. — (Do you really want to meet...?)
 Summary: "A child goes on an adventure to Australia to view kangaroos in the wild and learns how dangerous they can be when fighting over mates"— Provided by publisher.
 Audience: K to grade 3.
 ISBN 978-1-60753-734-2 (library binding) —
 ISBN 978-1-60753-838-7 (ebook)
 ISBN 978-1-68152-008-7 (paperback)
 1. Kangaroos—Juvenile literature. 2. Australia—Juvenile literature. I. Fabbri, Daniele, 1978– illustrator.
II. Title.
 QL737.M35M45 2016
 599.2'22—dc23   2014036507

Editor   Rebecca Glaser
Designer   Kathleen Petelinsek

Printed in the United States of America at Corporate Graphics in North Mankato, Minnesota.

HC 10 9 8 7 6 5 4 3 2 1
PB 10 9 8 7 6 5 4 3 2 1

ABOUT THE AUTHOR

Cari Meister is the author of more than 120 books for children, including the *Tiny* (Penguin Books for Young Readers) series and *Snow White and the Seven Dogs* (Scholastic, 2014). She lives in Evergreen, Colorado, with her husband, John, four sons, one horse, and one dog. You can visit Cari online at *www.carimeister.com*.

ABOUT THE ILLUSTRATOR

Daniele Fabbri was born in Ravenna, Italy, in 1978. He graduated from Istituto Europeo di Design in Milan, Italy, and started his career as a cartoon animator, storyboarder, and background designer for animated series. He has worked as a freelance illustrator since 2003, collaborating with international publishers and advertising agencies.

W hat's that you say? You really want to meet a kangaroo?

Kangaroos are cool. But did you know that kangaroos have enormous, razor-sharp claws that could easily slice through your skin?

Kangaroo attacks on humans are rare,
but they do happen from time to time.
They can leave some nasty scars.

What? You *still* want to meet a kangaroo?

You'll have to go to Australia. That's
the only place where kangaroos live in
the wild. They won't be hard to find.
Kangaroos are everywhere in Australia—
from the outback to the coastal areas.

Some kangaroos even live in cities, in open, grassy spaces. Let's go check the park. Make like a kangaroo and *hop* in the taxi.

See the roo bar on the front? It protects you from kangaroos. Kangaroos can weigh up to 200 pounds (91 kg). Do you know what that can do to a moving car?

Look at all the kangaroos! They don't *look* mean. The babies, called joeys, look cuddly in their mama's pouches. Joeys stay there and drink milk until they are strong enough to come out on their own.

GROOO

It's mating season. The males (called boomers) fight over the females (called flyers). A fight like this can be violent—and sometimes deadly. A kangaroo kicks with both legs at once, balancing on its large, strong tail. The kick is so powerful it can crush bones.

Kangaroos fight with everything they have—sharp claws, powerful legs, and teeth. Although kangaroos have extra-thick skin on their stomachs, when they "box," their stomachs can rip open. Eventually, one kangaroo will win.

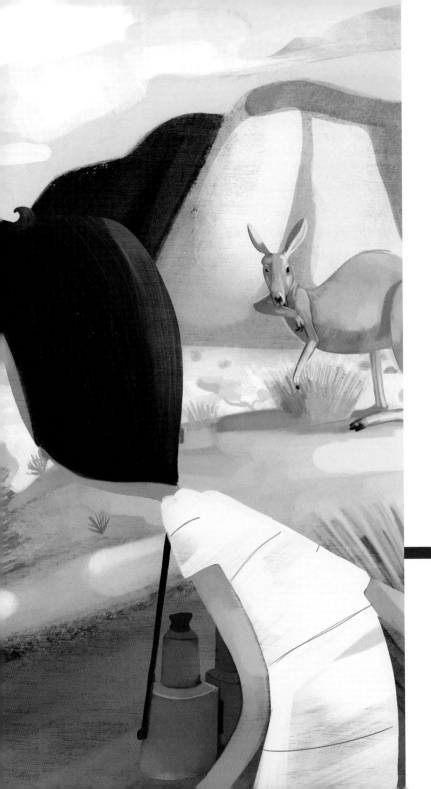

We can see even more kangaroos in the outback. But it's hot out here! Luckily, kangaroos can cool themselves. See that one out there licking his forearms? The saliva from his mouth helps cool him down.

Look through the binoculars. You will get a better view. What's that? Now you want to *feed* a kangaroo? You can't do that here.

You'll have to go to a wildlife sanctuary for that.

Wildlife sanctuaries are set up so visitors can get up close and personal with some mild-mannered kangaroos. Don't worry. These guys are tame.

Nice to meet you, roo!

AUSTRALIA

MAP KEY

● Eastern Grey Kangaroos

GLOSSARY

boomer A male kangaroo.

flyer A female kangaroo.

joey A baby kangaroo.

outback The part of Australia that is far away from cities.

saliva The liquid made in a person's or animal's mouth.

wildlife sanctuary A protected area of land set aside for animals to live in.

READ MORE

Bredeson, Carmen. **Kangaroos Up Close**. Berkeley Heights, NJ: Enslow, 2012.

Kras, Sara Louise. Kangaroos. Mankato, Minn.: Capstone Press, 2010.

Riggs, Kate. **Kangaroos**. Amazing Animals. Mankato, Minn.: Creative Education, 2012.

WEBSITES

Australia Zoo: Mammals: Kangaroos
http://www.australiazoo.com.au/our-animals/ amazing-animals/mammals/?mammal=kangaroos
View pictures and read facts about different species of kangaroos.

Fun Kangaroo Facts for Kids
http://www.sciencekids.co.nz/sciencefacts/animals/ kangaroo.html
Read fun trivia about kangaroos.

Kangaroo: National Geographic Kids
http://kids.nationalgeographic.com/animals/kangaroo.html
See how big a kangaroo is compared to common objects.

Ranger Rick: Red Kangaroos
http://www.nwf.org/Kids/Ranger-Rick/Animals/Mammals/ Red-Kangaroos.aspx
Read this article to learn more about this kangaroo species that lives in the deserts and outback of Australia.

Every effort has been made to ensure that these websites are appropriate for children. However, because of the nature of the Internet, it is impossible to guarantee that these sites will remain active indefinitely or that their contents will not be altered.